D1272187

100 Snowflakes

A Winter Counting Book

by Martha E. H. Rustad

AMICUS READERS 1 AMICUS INK

amicus readers

Say Hello to Amicus Readers.

You'll find our helpful dog, Amicus, chasing a ball—to let you know the reading level of a book.

1

Learn to Read

High frequency words and close photo-text matches introduce familiar topics and provide ample support for brand new readers.

2

Read Independently

Some repetition is mixed with varied sentence structures and a select amount of new vocabulary words are introduced with text and photo support.

3

Read to Know More

Interesting facts and engagin art and photos give fluent readers fun books both for reading practice and to learn about new topics.

Amicus Readers and Amicus Ink are imprints of Amicus
P.O. Box 1329, Mankato, MN 56002
www.amicuspublishing.us

Copyright © 2017 Amicus. International copyright reserved in all countries. No part of this book may be reproduced in any form without written permission from the publisher.

Library of Congress Cataloging-in-Publication Data
Names: Rustad, Martha E. H. (Martha Elizabeth Hillman), 1975- author.
Title: 100 snowflakes : a winter counting book / by Martha E. H. Rustad.
Other titles: One hundred snowflakes
Description: Mankato, MN : Amicus, [2017] | Series: 1, 2, 3 count with me |
  Audience: K to grade 3._ | Includes index.
Identifiers: LCCN 2015040337 (print) | LCCN 2015042605 (ebook) | ISBN
  9781607539186 (library binding) | ISBN 9781681521091 (pbk.) | ISBN
  9781681510422 (eBook)
Subjects: LCSH: Counting--Juvenile literature. | Snowflakes--Juvenile
  literature.
Classification: LCC QA113 .R885 2017 (print) | LCC QA113 (ebook) | DDC
  513.2/11--dc23
LC record available at http://lccn.loc.gov/2015040337

Photo Credits: All photos by iStock except: Corbis/JGI/Blend Images, 8, Corbis/Se De Burca, 20; Shutterstock/Sergey Novikov, 1, Lost Mountain Studio, 12-13, Sear Locke Photography, 23, Allies Interactive, 23, 24

Editor   Rebecca Glaser
Designer   Tracy Myers

Printed in the United States of America

HC 10 9 8 7 6 5 4 3 2 1
PB 10 9 8 7 6 5 4 3 2 1

Brr! Winter is here. Snowflakes are everywhere. Let's count one hundred snowflakes!

1, 2, 3, 4, 5,

Ten snowflakes land on a mitten. Snowflakes are tiny, frozen bits of water.

6, 7, 8, 9, 10

11, 12, 13, 14, 15,

We cut out 10 paper snowflakes. Each one looks different, just like real snowflakes. Now we've seen 20 snowflakes.

16, 17, 18, 19, 20

21, 22, 23, 24, 25

Ali sees 10 snowflakes on a present. We have counted 30 snowflakes.

26, 27, 28, 29, 30

Sam's scarf has 10 snowflakes.

Now we've seen 40 snowflakes.

31, 32, 33, 34, 35

66, 37, 38, 39, 40

41, 42, 43, 44, 45

12

Hala sees 10 snowflake cookies. They each have six points. Real snowflakes do, too! We have counted 50 snowflakes.

Emma counts 10 snowflakes on the bus window. Snowflakes fall from clouds. Now we've seen 60 snowflakes.

51, 52, 53, 54, 55

56, 57, 58, 59, 60

15

Marco hangs 10 snowflake ornaments.

61, 62, 63, 64, 65

We have counted 70 snowflakes.

66, 67, 68, 69, 70

Ten snowflake decorations stick to Jude's window. Now we've seen 80 snowflakes.

71, 72, 73, 74, 75

76, 77, 78, 79, 80

81, 82, 83, 84, 85

Nora has 10 snowflakes on her sweater. We have counted 90 snowflakes.

86, 87, 88, 89, 90

Miss Nelson counts 10 snowflake stickers. We mark the calendar. Now we've seen 100 snowflakes. How high can you count?

91, 92, 93, 94, 95

DECEMBER

SUNDAY	MONDAY	TUESDAY	WEDNESDAY	THURSDAY	FRIDAY	SATURDAY
		1	2	3	4	5
Hanukkah 6	7	8	9	10	11	12
13	14	15	16	17	18	19
20	21	22	23	Christmas Eve 24	Christmas 25	Kwanzaa Boxing Day (Canada) 26
27	28	29	30	New Year's Eve 31		

6, 97, 98, 99, 100

23

Count Again

Can you count all the way to one hundred?